White Noise
and Carousels.

Dear ▓▓▓

A pleasure meeting you. Thank you for the support.

[signature] 04/12/21

Efe Nakpodia

—thewrytr.

Photography by Arnaud Ele, www.arnaudele.com
Cover Design & Digital Production by Rasel Khondokar

Published by TheWrytr Books.

poetic forms inside

free verse

prose

tanka

haiku

senryu

sapphic

fibonacci

ALSO BY EFE NAKPODIA

White Noise and Love Angeles

REVIEWS

'Efe Nakpodia's delicately-crafted poetic vignettes are a joy to inhabit, conveying his love of language and deep knowledge of its power. In *White Noise and Carousels*, these individually stunning snapshots combine to create an atmospheric work greater even than the sum of its parts. Nakpodia invites his reader into a beautiful, almost cinematic universe full of love, pain, heartbreak and anxiety, which he captures with care and courage.' Henry James Garrett, Author of the best-selling book, *This Book Will Make You Kinder.* @henryjgarrett

'*White Noise and Carousels* is like catching your reflection in running water; certain poems and lines will make you still for a moment, in a world around us that flows so fast and uncontrollably. The world-building and imagery is transporting, which takes us on an inward journey that feels familiar. Reading the anthology, tapped into parts of myself; from memories and experiences to feelings that I rarely acknowledge or express. Yet with each poem, something else is brought to the surface in the most tender and comforting of ways. I'd recommend this stunning collection of poetry to any human, regardless of who they are or where they're from; to experience this beautiful and healing read.' Ashton Attzs, Illustrator and Painter @attzs_

'*White Noise and Carousels* puts and captures into words, the emotions and experiences, of what it is to feel. In this candid collection of poems and short stories, Efe makes himself vulnerable and in doing so, provides us with new insights on love and beauty,

fear and anxiety. Read aloud and listen to the lyrical and rhythmic tones of his words as they sing the images of emotion.'
Richard McVetis, Artist @richardmcvetis

'This book is so very precious. It takes you on a journey, exploring nuances within semantics. I got lost in the mishmash of the author's thoughts, but the kind of lost that is endearing and eventful. I found the randomness beautiful and free and I found the love mixed with the pain touching. This collection of poetry is something like I've never read before.' Eve De Haan, Artist @halfaroastchicken

'*White Noise and Carousels* immediately strikes you as a poetic memoir from a writer resolute in their life's journey. There is no illusion that this written sentiment is an effort to assuage the author's storied experiences with a beautiful juxtaposition of vulnerability and confidence. Whether structuring stanzas or prose, Efe never strays from being urbane in his delivery, employing a playful yet intimate tone that allures the reader. We are taken along a voyage of fear and hope, romance and insecurity... and tempted with a little faith. With this in mind, one can only look forward to the denouement that lies ahead in the third instalment by Efe Nakpodia.' Sean Verrall, Copywriter

ABOUT THE BOOK

White Noise and Carousels is a collection of short poetic
stories dealing with themes revolving around love and beauty,
fear and anxiety. It is the second edition of the White Noise
Anthology Series by Efe Nakpodia. Much like its
predecessor, this small book of dynamic poetry filled with
poignant emotions and stunning imagery, takes the reader on
an eventful journey of shifting scenes about *love and loss, pain
and anxiety, truth and healing.*

ABOUT THE AUTHOR

EFE NAKPODIA is an imagist poet and a storyteller on a mission to reinvent the way poetry is perceived and presented. Combining poetic text with various forms of multimedia from photography to woodwork, abstract design and fabric, Efe wants readers to see, feel, and fall in love with the complex simplicity of emotive language. He is the creator of the White Noise Anthology Series, and the editor of TheWrytr.com; a curated publication for poems and short stories. He lives in London, England.

FOREWORD

Are we slaves to our bodies? Every thought or feeling we will ever have, every action we will ever take originates from this organic shell of flesh and blood. It may be true that the eyes are windows to the soul, but what other secrets does the body hold? *White Noise and Carousels* by Efe Nakpodia is a poetry collection that delves deep into the intricate relationships that exist between our bodies, our souls, and a universe filled with contradictions.

Poetry is an apt tool for this type of inquiry. Rather than inundate the page with words, Nakpodia frequently employs the use of restraint. Several pieces take advantage of traditional Japanese forms like the haiku and senryū. Their sweet simplicity brings to mind the koan, those paradoxical Zen Buddhist breadcrumbs that lead the way to enlightenment. Nakpodia's love of evocative imagery and wordplay suffuses this collection with a buoyant torchlight of wit, earned by overcoming pain and discovering wisdom.

"You see, pain is a great counsellor that behaves like little specks of fallen stardust, lighting up cobblestone pathways in the dark, as we search for our elusive torch of purpose."

Stephen M. Tomic
Editor-in-chief, *The Junction*

AUTHOR'S NOTE

White Noise and Carousels is the second edition of the White Noise Series. Much like its predecessor, this collection of short poetic stories continues with themes I have now come to embrace as the inspirational forces behind my work: love, beauty, fear, and anxiety.

People may wonder why I choose to express feelings about fear, but most will not know that 'pain' has been a constant part of my world since the moment I arrived here. I was born with Sickle Cell Anaemia; an inherited chronic blood disorder that affects the red blood cells, causing excruciating pain at times. Living with this disease has not been easy to say the least. It has caused further medical complications that have affected my education, career, and most of my relationships.

So when I was rushed to hospital in a sickle crisis less than an hour into the new year of 2018, I knew that getting my first book published would be quite the challenge, as I had only finished the manuscript a few months earlier. I was given an emergency blood exchange transfusion and was hospitalised for over two weeks. But here's the thing: when I went into hospital, both of my hands were in good working order —but some time before I left, I had lost all use and sensation in my entire right hand.

I'd apparently suffered what's called a radial nerve palsy, and it would be another six months until I began to feel my fingers again. Imagine what that must have felt like for the right handed writer I believed myself to be. I can tell you —it was devastating! Nevertheless, I somehow found enough strength and determination to learn how to get by with my left hand, and a day after I returned home, I started writing what is now the book you are about to read.

That being said, it should come as no surprise that in this edition, I have focused on themes that deal with *love and loss, pain and anxiety, truth and healing.* I could probably sum up the entire collection in ten simple words: *sweet vulnerability, vision's surrealism, reality's illusion, perception's naivety, and beauty's allure.* But I would rather have you come to your own conclusions as to what the words in this little book of poetry mean to you.

Thank you for the time you took in making an investment in me and some of the many things that pass through my mind on a daily basis. As you peruse and flick through these pages, I hope the words fill you and your life with lots of love, lots of beauty, and enchanting romantic liaisons that are truly worthwhile, and hopefully worth remembering.

xoxo
Efe

White Noise
and Carousels.

—thewrytr.

CONTENTS

For you. Yes, you!

They say less is more,
so I learnt a thousand words,
and wrote this for you.

part one.

blindfolds.

fast cars and blindfolds.
an abandoned penthouse with
a boggled heart on a balustrade,
thinking thoughts in mid air.

Summersalts

Doing quite well, I am.
Landed on my feet, I did:
Landed on my elbows actually.
And the fall was quite a big one.
On the way down,
twists and twirls
sharpen'd the contrasts
of collage'd images;
life flashes between
eyes wide shut, shooting stars,
and plastic concrete.

Boing!

Landed on a rebound, I think...
and I am doing pretty well.
Or am I?
I must be;
for though I used
way more than nine
this time around,
I somehow managed to
land on both feet.
Falling upwards in love,
with back-flips and somersaults,
I managed to land squarely
on both feet, still throwing elbows.

jousting.

Demons on high horses
Battle with forbearance as
Humility runs out of patience,
Wounding arrogance with a
Fatal blow to the cojones,
Seconds before sundown,
At the height of the Ascots.

lumberjack.

our memories of
barefooted summers
run off with the forest
to cry over woodmilk,
like the ghosts of
felled rubber trees.

swing an axe
to cut a boxer short;
swing an axe, to show love
truncate the feelings we
left behind the chainsaw
in case things got better.
aren't we special now?

heartlesssleeves.

i can see your fears
leaking through the emoji
you frequently put on display;
and you would more than likely see
mine too, if it weren't for these
star-spangled distractions
i carefully work to put into play

Sixmyth.

i lose
my sixth
sense of pride
every time you
come around...
but it doesn't hurt,
not even for a
moment, because
you always love
the humiliation

dread.

if
we'd
stay'd true,
long enough
for us to become,
love would've stuck to our game plan
and hate would've taken one of its biggest losses,
for we would've blossom'd truly
and conquer'd our fear
of white noise
and all
the
dread

dread
feelings
travel through
your blue-blooded veins,
distorting emotions again:
wandering with my daydreams, venturing out in vain,
the pamper'd fingernails of time
run through memories;
follicles
of mind,
tick,
tock

innocence.

the look
on your face
engulf my eyes
in a portrait
of a story untold:
in empathy, i appear
to catch a glimpse of
your world, seconds
before the rain stiffen'd
your smile, stealing
your inner sense

Infatuatus.

I know I shouldn't and
I find it hard to resist.
Desire beckons, but
discipline loathes
temptation.

Show me where to hide
when seduction becomes
suspicious —in my
sweet dreams, I swear
I'll make new revisions.

Infatuation found lust, but
love may still call its bluff.
She knows I shouldn't,
and I find it hard to resist;
her gaze, her blush:
my demons.

White Noise and Jack Russells

Cute as a bundle of four legged joy, you would be forgiven for not quite understanding my tremulous reaction as she came running straight towards me.

As cunning as a fox would have been a more fitting expression for her current disguise but today, she's turned an adorable little Russell into a man's worst enemy. She jumps on my lap and stares knowingly into my eyes, angling for a pat on the back. All warm and cuddly on the outside, she knew that I knew exactly who she was beneath her ruffled coat of brown and white fur. Even in the form of a fun-loving canine with a taste for unbridled mischief, her sweet tooth was betrayed by the way she paused to lap up a drink of spilled milk and sour honey.

I fed her a few pup-peronies, then I secretly wished for a way to make her stop growing. You may laugh at my demise because you still do not understand why, but know this for certain: her bite will push the fear of God deep into your flesh, sending shivers up and down your funny bones.

She took me for a run up the hill to fetch a pail of crabs in a barrel and not before long, I was at a loss for words as to why I couldn't get out of the box she'd managed to lure me into. The more the guests talked about how fond of her they were, the more I found myself unable to take off her cheeky little mask. But when she sat down to give me a paw in a subtle show of dogged deception,

I made it a point to simply press pause and miraculously, she withdrew into thin air.

Still, as long as I continue to hold onto these awkward sticks and fretful frisbees, I know that fear will return soon enough to play fetch with me and my stream of thoughts, as we dream of flying colours, and floating castles in the sky.

part two.

a Senryu, for you.

Somewhere in her eyes,
in her ogling desires,
he has lost himself.

Somewhere in his mind,
in his cold box of fire,
she has found herself.

Somewhere in the night,
in the music of the lyre,
they have lost themselves.

Somewhere in these isles,
in their story—denial,
you have found yourself.

Sweet Dreams and Gang Bangers

I've been out of it
for a minute or two.
Choices assault my frontal lobe
in the middle of a crossroad as
past decisions drive by,
three guns blazing.

I've been out of sync
for an hour or two.
Stray bullets whizz past my affections as
slow emotions begin to run for cover.
Three desert eagles and a hole in the ground:
meerkat feelings flee and stay,
hidden for a fortnight.

I've been out of it
for a week or two now.
A voice in the Kalahari whispers
scenes from a fractured future:
conflicted spirits search
a hedonistic utopia filled empty.

Voids and vessels, angled circles,
snapping selfies with grief,
sweet dreams and gang bangers.

boxes and algorithms.

Patterns in,
Form patterns out,
Per form, slash pattern.

Patterns within,
Form patterns without:
Formulaic forms,
Oscillating patterns.

quiqmaffs.

my heart
and my head
aren't adding up:
they steadily subtract
from one another,
multiplying misunderstandings,
strengthening divisions

Persian Eagle

remember
when we rode
on the wings of the
southern wind and
listened to the ocean
call out the sun?
you knew we'd soar
right down to earth,
so you just smiled
when you heard me say
angel, i'm not brave

Wolf On a Duck's Back

Haphazardly half-hearted,
We spill milk over wine
Glasses half full, and cry
Wolf onto a duck's back.

Amid such stifling conundrums,
Sand stormed silhouettes
Surround our glowing temples,
Safeguarding precious halos
Falling deeper into ruin.

Like water being poured into
Empty hourglasses, in time,
We too shall rise to the challenge:
Quenching our thirst for things
Without meaning, with all things
Bright, and beautiful.

heroine.

when you walked through
the gliding doors gleaming,
you took it so far away from me,
the barmaid tried to catch it,
just so i could breathe again

Death Can Pass Over

Tears draped in water colours
adorn your high cheek zone like
chiselled works of broken art.

I fall deep into your countenance,
as kaleidoscopic emoji escape your
looking glass, painting blood on a
bland door: but no angel of death
can pass over our love and not
double take our fate at least once,
once upon a twilight.

woodpulp.

jealousy
will unfold like
a rebellious origami
the moment these sensus
begin to woo the fans

Breaks In a Cocoon.

In the throes of a mean black hole,
I keep the faith to face Apophis.

Shredding auld skin for
alt new beginnings,
love's light shimmers through
as dawn breaks in a cocoon;
flaunting wings of a renaissance,
floating outward towards relief.

part three.

At Home With The Woes

Loneliness spent time on folly
and told her to keep the change.
 An empty gesture, fulfilled.
If a grain of sand is a currency in love,
how many hearts does an hourglass buy?

As moonwalking hours pass by,
currents of a recurring dream plot
 to keep her flowing inward,
accompanied by the woes of a recluse,
 living off an ebb on the low.

Poledancing.

she said life is but
a game of half-truths
where everything is and
isn't, at the same time

i said if home is where
the heart is, let's go
somewhere far...
somewhere, the mind isn't

Behind, The Pixels.

she wore a curiously expensive
fur coat that night, but closest
to the skin around her neck was
a thin layer of woven fleece:
a lamb in a wolf's cloak,
silently bleating.

monoglots + polymaths.

i had fallen for her and all that she knew:
a polyandrous polymath she was, and
her riant voice bewitched the vodka in me;
the patsy monoglot

when.

she loves to lay, i love to lie.
she told me hers, i told her lies.
i love the tears, she loves to cry.
she asked me when, i don't know why.

she loves to lay, i love to lie.
i'm pretty sure, she's pretty shy.
she said good day, i said goodbye.
she asked me when, i don't know why.

she loves to lay, i love to lie.
she wants the moon, i want july.
she fell in love, i'm not the guy.
she asked me when, i don't know why.

she loves to lay, i love to lie.
she sang a song; a lullaby.
i saw her fears, and then we died.
she asked me when, i don't know why.

culting.

A voice over a pulpit:
Wrinkled notes of inked wood pulp
Rustle at the hands of woolly faces,
Furrowed by the creases:
Welcome to the fold.

Seconds.

You came after me,
Seconds after I fell inside
A hole without a rabbit,
So it belongs to you;
My heart, for the rescue.

Hauteculture.

Let's sow these wild seeds.
Bury them in mindful hearts,
Then wait for the bloom:
We'll know them by their petals,
And prejudice shall be pruned.

au courant

i am

the
carbon
copy
of an
astral idea
forged in
the mind of
the all,

out pictured
here in the flesh
as an original
expression of a
six dimensional
thought

furnished with
kaleidoscopic
rays of light
that reveal
precisely who
i am;

un hologramme
conscient

Small Toes and Shin Bones

I had been searching and stumbling over obstacles and objects in the dark. Habitually hurting small toes and shin bones on things my eyes could not yet see, I learned to embrace the pain. I held it close, as if she was the only one for me —my stupidly stubborn soulmate.

After all, everyone's pain is as intimate and as exclusive to them as the patch of earth all trees stem from. But beneath that spot where tree meets earth, right there in the depths of a deep darkness, its pain spreads its roots far and wide; far beyond the confined footprint of its outer canopy. And what cannot be seen, cannot be judged. Yet we judge, nevertheless. You see, pain is a great counsellor that behaves like little specks of fallen stardust, lighting up cobblestone pathways in the dark, as we search for our elusive torch of purpose.

Slowly but intently, I found myself one of these rare torches and I was no longer afraid in the dark. And I didn't need any help from Prometheus either, for this torch had my name engraved into it. So I alone could've found it, and I alone had the power to command it. From that moment onward, I would simply speak the words the way they were spoken in the beginning, and I could navigate through the map of my own life with great poise and bold determination.

Endowed with this new gift of mind, I'd skip over objects here and spin around obstacles there, keeping small toes and shin bones perfectly safe and sound. You see, for every idea that has made it possible for new things to become possible, a lightbulb was taken from a place in the dark, where pain is always an enlightening companion.

Of what use is a candle in the sun? Can light shed any more light on what is already very well lit? Remember, the commanding words were 'let there be light'. So with a little faith and an ounce of some fruit bearing pain, get out there and face dark fears squarely. Like right now, in the living dead of night.

part four.

Crayons and Twilight

Colour in nightfall,
as the sun's rays leave the sky,
with pink and yellow.

playtime.

i couldn't
wait for you
to finish playing
the waiting game,
so i exercised
a little patience
instead

wish.

i wish they'd come out;
these lustful thoughts in my heart:
the vices they bring,
and the obsessions they leave;
i wish they'd just fall, right out

rebellion.

made
you a promise
i still intend to keep
but through all my blunders,
you stay blindly in love,
as if by mistake, i rebelled
against my own truth
and found you,
waiting

eyed ears.

i wanted to be
as close to you,
but i wasn't
as pure as blood
stained glass:
wrestling shame
on bended knees,
i close my eyes,
and you're all ears

mirrored.

your flaws imitate
perfection's disguise:
a seductive deception garbed
in fanciful delusions of devils
and details that stand out,
wishing they didn't exist

hooked.

picture the way
you look at things:
catch a glimpse
with your hooked
line of thought.

i stand by your
riverbank, baiting
pin pointed views,
fishing, for a new
perspective.

cuddles.

Father,
forgive me
but you know
i have emotions;
in beginning was
her mother and
all of the nemesis.

saturated by the
colours that fell
off another feeling;
cuddled pillows for
a healing —as high
as i've ever been:

i sang this solo
for so long.

Button With Your Left

press
against
my belly
button
with your
left nipple

can you
feel it?
honey,
that's
yin yang

exNihilo.

reality stems from
the negative copy of
a graphical thought,
caught in a paradoxical
loop of spatial consciousness:

an illusion, doomed to be
brought to an abrupt end by
a derisory version of itself,
where only a fragment of the
original idea ever really existed.

part five.

zephyr.

Summer's hangover
falls gently before autumn:
she leaves, blown away.

Schönheit.

she said,
beauty hides
in plain sight,
virtually unknown:
a blinding elegance
floating through
space-time,
searching.

i said,
beauty is
something i've
never seen before,
but when we do meet,
i'll look, so beautiful
may see me too,
for the very first time.

Poise and Impulse

she held it
close to my chest,
pressed against buttons
on a long sleeve, pulsating

a heart over a cuff link;
a spade in a club with a
diamond and forever,
toying with a cast die,
playing her cards right

spacebar.

i pushed the sky
and she opened up
in real time

a keystroke,
her frequency;
i hear them travel
through the ether:
between every word,
i find her, lurking

Anima.

Spirits hide within the ether,
Whispering wavelike incantations
Telepathically: like invisible ushers,
Welcoming a nude awakening.

frames.

intentions,
intense incentives
burnish the frame of
 the mood we're in,
letting go briefly,
 as they come
 to our senses

crawl.

Searching for a blemish somewhere along skin,
fingers crawl to a halt on a beauty spot
bound to bring clarity to flesh and freckles,
dabbed with all your stains.

Pillars, and Salt.

The way you look
Back and forthright
Through my optics;

Like a pendulum
Swung from
Love's taste in
Lustful illusions:
Hung up on a feeling,
Once upon a time.

titan.

help
me find
a way
through the
frozen lanes of
iceberg way:
you are the
driving force
behind my
stirring will to
live and die
warm-hearted

A Faithful Obsession.

My thoughts are plagued by the image of my desires playing hide and seek with my beliefs. They've been on this voyage since knee high, when uncertainty didn't exist. I never questioned the source of their intentions. I simply wanted to see what they saw by the crossroads overseas, where the waves were said to be surreal. A puerile naivety perhaps, but it was mine, nonetheless.

Day after day, I'd sit by the harbour with my dreams on a limb and quietly dandle, until they'd lull me to sleep. I'd seen their world a million times before so, many things weren't impossible. Picture a place where the things you imagine could be made manifest the moment you fed them your purest emotions. I had made multiple trips by now, so in reality, anything was virtually possible. In my young mind, doubt was akin to the devil at the time; they both didn't exist. Until my Adam's apple began to grow... and then, it fell—quite far from the tree. I wanted all the shiny things the lights had to offer, but Mama and Papa had made blue prints of their own. They'd made plans to go backwards, bringing forth the blackout.

When a loss creates far fetched distortions ferried from wells a thousand miles away, does pain become a friend, or does it remain famously fiendish? If it weren't for these familial bonds and extramarital blindfolds, my watercoloured tears would've found an answer by now. Loneliness is colour-blind in the presence of a rainbow, and I'd fallen to a place of great depression, envious of Solitude, and her quaint expressions. Who'd been writing the script for my existence up until their separation? Every time I had to play my part, I often wondered if they could sense how very disappointed I was in the role they'd carved out for me. I didn't seem to fit with the rest of the cast so in truth, I felt a castaway —surrounded with nothing but white noise and a curious fear of the future. But as timorous as I may have appeared to most on the outside, courage and desire conspired to reign over the main features of my interior design. So, I challenged failure to a game of truth or dare, but he was too scared of taking risks. I asked freedom if she'd found herself yet, but she lacked the vision to look within.

What kind of a place is this? A place where happiness plots jealously against joyfulness? I had eleven hundred and one questions and I desperately needed some answers, but no one cared enough to give me a tip of the faintest clue. At about a quarter mile from this moment in time, I remember thinking they were all a bunch of selfish cowards... but then it occurred to me that it was quite possible that they were also searching for the same things I had come in search of: a little laughter, some contentment, and a lifetime with peace of mind. I had started to lose all hope but patience couldn't care less about such a loss, for she knew that being hopeful wasn't what was needed. Patience knew with an unwavering certainty that what I needed was a single dose of good old faith! An enduring faith that possessed enough wisdom to see past the ills of a present moment, into the thrills of an elaborate future. As time passed and blame retreated to the more mature corners of my being, I found solace in the knowledge that empathy and I wore the same pair of ragged brogue shoes. I learned to show gratitude for all the memories of the motion pictures my eyes had captured along the watery lanes of this sinful odyssey—life!

It was a strange feeling that day by the appointed place, and he came just in time. I'd arrived at Destiny's Port where my most original self was waiting with my name on a screen in the palm of his hand. I stood still, in awesome tranquility, face to face with the 'I' that I am; thankful for this gift of life, and a faithful obsession with Alpha's Omega. My thoughts had been plagued by the image of my desires playing hide and seek with my dreams. They'd been on this voyage since knee high, when they could sail to places uncertainty could never reach. I never questioned the depths of their integrity, for I so wanted to see what they saw by the crossroads, overseas. A puerile fantasy it was, perhaps, but it was mine nonetheless. A young man's story of all time, ending here, as it once begun.

THE END

But wait, there's one more!

Daydreams.

Between a rock and a fountain,
I find my dreams
lost upon a face and a time,
gridlocked in haute couture.

Remember when beauty evaporated
into a vision in the clouds and
hid behind the sun until she fell,
morphing into snowflakes?

The three faces of the
mighty Matterhorn remind me of
a blissful avalanche, and the day
some hell and high waters fell
through my sweet dreams.

In the rumblings
of a flowing mountain,
I stood still and heard your voice
running circles around the walls in
my veins, then day broke, and
all my dreams came true.

—thewrytr.

MORE REVIEWS

'*White Noise and Carousels* is a twisting romance between faith and fear, reality and illusion... *Alice in Wonderland* vibes. Clever wordplay and very engaging to read. A multidimensional trip, capturing a scope on the feelings of the human experience. The profound imagery creates entire worlds in just a few words. My personal favourite is '**Au Courant**'; I want it written on the walls of my house.' Aicha Thérèse, Spoken-word Artist @aichatherese

'I would like to share a few thoughts with you on one particular piece that stood out to me personally: **Small Toes and Shin Bones**. This piece really touched my heart especially as someone who has been dealing with putting herself out there and really going after the things God has laid on my heart to do. The fear of the unknown and the fear of failure has crippled me many times just as you have perfectly painted it – like 'stumbling over objects in the dark and hitting my small toes and shin bones on things my eyes could not yet see'. What is it about fear that has such a profound crippling effect and at the same time is able to make us feel so comfortable? This piece has reminded me once again that yes, although fear and pain is something that is part of me and has accompanied me during many stages of my life, it is not actually guiding me through this life— my purpose is. 'Can light shed any more light on what is already well lit?' My answer would be no, but I still want to thank you for reigniting the {little} light that is within me.'
Heidi Agyapong, Writer @via.herthoughts

'I have absolutely loved reading it. Your story is so inspiring. It all has a very personal feel to it which had me captivated pretty much instantly. Nothing about your poetry is wishy washy, which as a preference I absolutely love. And also how you structure your poems. There's a juxtaposition I like too, as there's your unique style of writing and then occasionally you throw in something a bit longer. Truly absolutely love your work. So inspired by it and your story.' Lucy Barnes, Blogger @bookcaseofbarnes

'I've read a fair bit of poetry and short stories in verse but this was something really special. It was absolutely breathtaking. I particularly loved 'Persian Eagle', 'Mirrored' and 'Titan'. You have produced a beautiful piece of poetic literature and you should be so so proud. I wrote a short story in verse some years ago now—you've inspired me to possibly go down the poetry route again.'
Ekaterina Botziou, Author @ekaterinabotziou

'*White Noise and Carousels* is a gift, a real beauty of a gift... for all of us, and I'll explain why. When I read Efe's notes at the beginning—before we delve into his poetic world—the poet informs us that he wanted to express 'fear' or rather, face it (which he does beautifully). However, what I experienced above any other emotion was deep surrender and love: surrender and love for words, imagery and play; love for memories or rather, the beauty of imagination and life. It seemed to me like the voice of an adult and a child, mixed together in poetic honesty, freedom, musicality, coolness and style... and highly relatable. I was transported, laughed and smiled. There were moments where I felt the author's pain, his moments of loneliness, and his need for healing... and with this, he was ironically healing my thoughts and mind with his words. That is why I say it is a gift. I have my favourite poems already that have left imprints on my mind because the imagery, although proverbial, is yet so clear and just sincerely beautiful. I loved it.'
Adébayo Bolaji, Artist @adebayobolaji

MORE FROM THIS AUTHOR

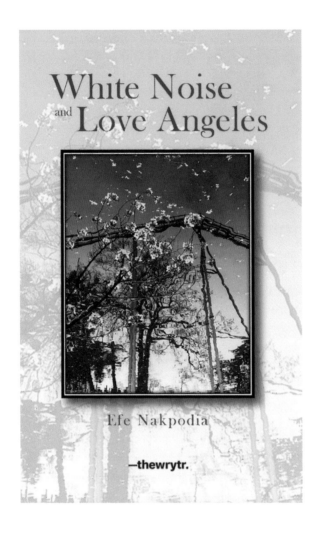

Printed in Great Britain
by Amazon